T0302446

Celebrate

Asking God to Grow My Character

The Journey Continues

PARTICIPANT'S GUIDE 6

John Baker is the founder of Celebrate Recovery®, a ministry started at Saddleback Church. It is estimated that over the last 25 years more than 1.5 million people have gone through this Christ-centered recovery program. There are currently over 27,000 churches that have weekly Celebrate Recovery meetings.

John has been on staff since Celebrate Recovery started. He has served as the Pastor of Membership, the Pastor of Ministries, and is currently the Pastor of Saddleback Church's Signature Ministries. He is also serving as one of the nine Elder Pastors at Saddleback. John is a nationally known speaker and trainer in helping churches start Celebrate Recovery ministries.

John's writing accomplishments include Celebrate Recovery's *The Journey Begins* Curriculum, *Life's Healing Choices*, the *Celebrate Recovery Study Bible* (general editor), and *The Landing* and *Celebration Place* (coauthor). John's newest books are *Your First Step to Celebrate Recovery* and *The Celebrate Recovery Devotional* (coauthor).

John and his wife Cheryl, the cofounder of Celebrate Recovery, have been married for more than four decades and have served together in Celebrate Recovery since the beginning. They have two adult children, Laura and Johnny, and five grandchildren.

Johnny Baker has been on staff at Celebrate Recovery since 2004 and has been the Pastor of Celebrate Recovery at Saddleback Church since 2012. As an adult child of an alcoholic who chose to become an alcoholic himself, Johnny is passionate about breaking the cycle of dysfunction in his family and helping other families find the tools that will lead to healing and openness. He knows that because of Jesus Christ, and by continuing to stay active in Celebrate Recovery, Maggie, Chloe, and Jimmy—his three children—will never see him drink. Johnny is a nationally recognized speaker, trainer, and teacher of Celebrate Recovery. He is a coauthor of the *Celebrate Recovery Daily Devotional*, *Celebration Place*, and *The Landing*, and is an associate editor of the *Celebrate Recovery Study Bible*. He has been married since 2000 to his wife Jeni, who serves alongside him in Celebrate Recovery.

Celebrate Recovery®

Asking God to Grow My Character

PARTICIPANT'S GUIDE 6

The Journey Continues

NEW CURRICULUM!

A recovery program based on eight principles from the Beatitudes

JOHN BAKER & JOHNNY BAKER

FOREWORD BY RICK WARREN

ZONDERVAN®

ZONDERVAN

Asking God to Grow My Character
Copyright © 2016 by John and Johnny Baker

This title is also available as a Zondervan ebook.

Requests for information should be addressed to:
Zondervan, 3900 *Sparks Dr. SE, Grand Rapids, Michigan 49546*

ISBN 978-0-310-13148-9 (softcover)
ISBN 978-0-310-13149-6 (ebook)

All Scripture quotations, unless otherwise indicated, are taken from The Holy Bible, New International Version®, NIV®. Copyright © 1973, 1978, 1984, 2011 by Biblica, Inc.® Used by permission of Zondervan. All rights reserved worldwide. www.Zondervan.com. The "NIV" and "New International Version" are trademarks registered in the United States Patent and Trademark Office by Biblica, Inc.®

Scripture quotations marked GNT are taken from the *Good News Translation (Today's English Version), Second Edition*. Copyright ©1992 by American Bible Society. Used by permission.

Scripture quotations marked NCV are taken from the *New Century Version*®. © 2005 by Thomas Nelson. Used by permission. All rights reserved.

Scripture quotations marked NLT are taken from the *Holy Bible*, New Living Translation. © 1996, 2004, 2007, 2013 by Tyndale House Foundation. Used by permission of Tyndale House Publishers, Inc., Carol Stream, Illinois 60188. All rights reserved.

Scripture quotations marked TLB are taken from *The Living Bible*. Copyright © 1971 by Tyndale House Publishers, Inc., Wheaton, Illinois 60188. All rights reserved.

Any Internet addresses (websites, blogs, etc.) and telephone numbers in this book are offered as a resource. They are not intended in any way to be or imply an endorsement by Zondervan, nor does Zondervan vouch for the content of these sites and numbers for the life of this book.

All rights reserved. No part of this publication may be reproduced, stored in a retrieval system, or transmitted in any form or by any means—electronic, mechanical, photocopy, recording, or any other—except for brief quotations in printed reviews, without the prior permission of the publisher.

Cover design: Brand Navigation
Cover photography: 123rf.com

First Printing May 2016 / Printed in the United States of America

Contents

Foreword

The best known ministry at Saddleback Church—that is going to last for easily 100, maybe 200 years—started when a guy, who was a drunk, came to me with a 13-page letter. And that ministry is called Celebrate Recovery®.

Now, let me just put this in perspective. This may be Saddleback's greatest contribution to the world. Over 20,000 people have completed the step studies at Saddleback's Celebrate Recovery. Over three and a half million people worldwide have gone through a Celebrate Recovery step study.

Right now, around the world, 27,000 churches are using Saddleback's ministry called Celebrate Recovery—27,000 churches! It is so successful that Celebrate Recovery is the official recovery program in 44 state and federal prison systems. It has been translated into 20 different languages.

Do you think John Baker, when he came to see me in my office many years ago and said, "I've got an idea for a ministry, Pastor Rick," imagined it would be affecting three and a half million people in 27,000 churches? No. You have no idea what God wants to do through you. You may have the next big ministry idea. You may have the next Celebrate Recovery dwelling in you—a ministry that could be started and reproduced to bless the whole world. One guy, out of his own pain, starts a ministry that now affects tens of thousands of churches and millions of people.

Rick Warren

(Excerpted from Pastor Warren's talk at Angel Stadium on Saddleback's 35th anniversary)

Introduction

Let us examine our ways and test them, and let us return to the L*ORD. (Lamentations 3:40)*

Welcome to the next step study in *The Journey Continues.* You are about to revisit Principle 4 and all it entails. Remember, Principle 4 says, "Openly examine and confess my faults to myself, to God, and to someone I trust." Here in Participant's Guide 6, *Asking God to Grow My Character,* you will once again dig into the work of Principle 4.

You'll begin by taking a look at what makes, and what makes you, a good sponsor and servant leader. You will look at the truth you have discovered about yourself from prior step study groups, and then you will begin a fresh, new Spiritual Inventory. There are three brand new lessons on the Inventory to help you get writing again. There's even a brand new worksheet, called "Pro's from My Inventory," designed to help you keep track of all the good things you have done and that God has done through you since starting Celebrate Recovery. If you have a copy of a past inventory, you'll want to have it close by.

This is a chance for you to dig deeper into existing recovery issues and any new issues that have arisen since completing a *The Journey Begins* group. Remember all of the victory you experienced from your initial inventory, and expect God to do great things in your life during this one, too.

John Baker
Johnny Baker

The Road to Recovery

Eight Principles Based on the Beatitudes

By Pastor Rick Warren

1. **R**ealize I'm not God. I admit that I am powerless to control my tendency to do the wrong thing and that my life is unmanageable. (Step 1)
   "Happy are those who know that they are spiritually poor."
   (Matthew 5:3)
2. **E**arnestly believe that God exists, that I matter to Him, and that He has the power to help me recover. (Step 2)
   "Happy are those who mourn, for they shall be comforted."
   (Matthew 5:4)
3. **C**onsciously choose to commit all my life and will to Christ's care and control. (Step 3)
   "Happy are the meek." (Matthew 5:5)
4. **O**penly examine and confess my faults to myself, to God, and to someone I trust. (Steps 4 and 5)
   "Happy are the pure in heart." (Matthew 5:8)
5. **V**oluntarily submit to any and all changes God wants to make in my life and humbly ask Him to remove my character defects. (Steps 6 and 7)
   "Happy are those whose greatest desire is to do what God requires." (Matthew 5:6)
6. **E**valuate all my relationships. Offer forgiveness to those who have hurt me and make amends for harm I've done to others when possible, except when to do so would harm them or others. (Steps 8 and 9)
   "Happy are the merciful." (Matthew 5:7)
   "Happy are the peacemakers." (Matthew 5:9)
7. **R**eserve a time with God for self-examination, Bible reading, and prayer in order to know God and His will for my life and to gain the power to follow His will. (Steps 10 and 11)
8. **Y**ield myself to God to be used to bring this Good News to others, both by my example and my words. (Step 12)
   "Happy are those who are persecuted because they do what God requires." (Matthew 5:10)

Twelve Steps and Their Biblical Comparisons*

1. We admitted we were powerless over our addictions and compulsive behaviors, that our lives had become unmanageable. I know that nothing good lives in me, that is, in my sinful nature.

   "For I know that good itself does not dwell in me, that is, in my sinful nature. For I have the desire to do what is good, but I cannot carry it out." (Romans 7:18)

2. We came to believe that a power greater than ourselves could restore us to sanity.

   "For it is God who works in you to will and to act in order to fulfill his good purpose." (Philippians 2:1)

3. We made a decision to turn our lives and our wills over to the care of God.

   "Therefore, I urge you, brothers and sisters, in view of God's mercy, to offer your bodies as a living sacrifice, holy and pleasing to God—this is your true and proper of worship." (Romans 12:1)

4. We made a searching and fearless moral inventory of ourselves.

   "Let us examine our ways and test them, and let us return to the LORD." (Lamentations 3:40)

5. We admitted to God, to ourselves, and to another human being the exact nature of our wrongs.

   "Therefore confess your sins to each other and pray for each other so that you may be healed." (James 5:16)

6. We were entirely ready to have God remove all these defects of character.

   "Humble yourselves before the LORD, and he will lift you up." (James 4:10)

7. We humbly asked Him to remove all our shortcomings.

   "If we confess our sins, he is faithful and will forgive us our sins and purify us from all unrighteousness." (1 John 1:9)

8. We made a list of all persons we had harmed and became willing to make amends to them all.

   "Do to others as you would have them do to you." (Luke 6:31)

9. We made direct amends to such people whenever possible, except when to do so would injure them or others.

   "Therefore, if you are offering your gift at the altar and there remember that your brother or sister has something against you, leave your gift there in front of the altar. First go and be reconciled to them; then come and offer your gift." (Matthew 5:23–24)

10. We continued to take personal inventory and when we were wrong, promptly admitted it.

    "So, if you think you are standing firm, be careful that you don't fall!" (1 Corinthians 10:12)

11. We sought through prayer and meditation to improve our conscious contact with God, praying only for knowledge of His will for us, and power to carry that out.

    "Let the message of Christ dwell among you richly." (Colossians 3:16)

12. Having had a spiritual experience as the result of these steps, we try to carry this message to others and practice these principles in all our affairs.

    "Brothers and sisters, if someone is caught in a sin, you who live by the Spirit should restore that person gently. But watch yourselves, or you also may be tempted." (Galatians 6:1)

* Throughout this material, you will notice several references to the Christ-centered 12 Steps. Our prayer is that Celebrate Recovery will create a bridge to the millions of people who are familiar with the secular 12 Steps (we acknowledge the use of some material from the 12 Suggested Steps of Alcoholics Anonymous) and in so doing, introduce them to the one and only true Higher Power, Jesus Christ. Once they begin that relationship, asking Christ into their hearts as Lord and Savior, true healing and recovery can begin!

Serenity Prayer

God, grant me the serenity
to accept the things I cannot change,
the courage to change the things I can,
and the wisdom to know the difference.
Living one day at a time,
enjoying one moment at a time;
accepting hardship as a pathway to peace;
taking, as Jesus did,
this sinful world as it is,
not as I would have it;
trusting that You will make all things right
if I surrender to Your will;
so that I may be reasonably happy in this life
and supremely happy with You forever in the next.
Amen.

Reinhold Niebuhr

Celebrate Recovery's Small Group Guidelines

The following five guidelines will ensure that your small group is a safe place. They need to be read at the beginning of every meeting.

1. Keep your sharing focused on your own thoughts and feelings. Limit your sharing to three to five minutes.
2. There is NO cross talk. Cross talk is when two individuals engage in conversation excluding all others. Each person is free to express his or her feelings without interruptions.
3. We are here to support one another, not "fix" another.
4. Anonymity and confidentiality are basic requirements. What is shared in the group stays in the group. The only exception is when someone threatens to injure themselves or others.
5. Offensive language has no place in a Christ-centered recovery group.

Lesson 7

Sponsor

Principle 4: Openly examine and confess my faults to myself, to God, and to someone I trust.

"Happy are the pure in heart." (Matthew 5:8)

Step 4: We made a searching and fearless moral inventory of ourselves.

"Let us examine our ways and test them, and let us return to the Lord." (Lamentations 3:40)

Please begin your time together by reading "The Fourth Step, Day 90" from the *Celebrate Recovery Daily Devotional.*

The road to recovery is not meant to be traveled alone. As we discovered in *The Journey Begins,* we actually needed three major relationships. First and most important is our relationship with Jesus Christ. In addition, we found that everyone needs relationships with the people in their recovery group. Last, everyone needs a relationship with a sponsor and/or accountability partner/team. Identifying a sponsor and/or accountability partner/team was especially important before beginning Principles 4 through 6, in which we worked on getting right with God, ourselves, and others.

Principle 4 is all about getting rid of our "truth decay." It's all about coming clean! Proverbs 15:14 tells us, "A wise person is hungry for the truth, while a fool feeds on trash" (NLT).

Are you ready to feed on the truth about your life? Well then, it's time to take out the trash! That trash can get pretty heavy at times, so we learned in *The Journey Begins* that we shouldn't handle it alone. We all needed a genuine mentor, coach, or in recovery terms, a sponsor and/or an accountability partner/team.

Now that we are in *The Journey Continues*, we will find a few new facets of this lesson. First, it's time for us to step out and sponsor other people who are beginning their recovery journey. Also, we may find that we have stepped away from our sponsors or accountability partner/team and need to find new people to support us on the road to recovery. Here are some qualities to look for in the people we need to support us and to provide for the people we will help.

On a personal note, I would strongly suggest that everyone has both a sponsor and an accountability partner/team. Why? Because if we only have one person we can turn to when temptation comes, we could be in trouble. What if we can't reach our sponsor at the moment we are fighting relapse? If we have both a sponsor and accountability partner/team, our chances of getting help increase. Also, I have seen many situations between a sponsor and the person being sponsored become a very unhealthy, dependent relationship. Remember, we are to place that dependency on Christ's power, not our sponsor's finite power.

—John Baker

SPONSOR

S—Servant leader

Sponsors should not be dictators. They lead from the freedom they have experienced in living out the steps and principles.

"For even the Son of Man did not come to be served, but to serve, and to give his life as a ransom for many." (Mark 10:45)

P—Power comes from God, not from the sponsor

We need to keep our relationships healthy. As sponsors, it's important to make sure we are giving godly advice. This is why having accountability partners is such a good idea. They can help us make sure that our sponsors are doing the same with us.

"So that your faith might not rest on human wisdom, but on God's power." (1 Corinthians 2:5)

O—Open to share their recovery journey

Sponsors need to be transparent. Remember, we are all works in progress. Sponsors need to be persons of integrity.

"Whoever walks in integrity walks securely, but whoever takes crooked paths will be found out." (Proverbs 10:9)

> *Integrity means that if our private life was suddenly exposed, we'd have no reason to be ashamed or embarrassed. Integrity means our outward life is consistent with our inner convictions.*
>
> —Billy Graham

N—Nonjudgmental

Our role as a sponsor is not to judge those we sponsor, but to guide them by encouraging them and by challenging them. Sponsors need to be role models.

"Don't judge others, or you will be judged. You will be judged in the same way that you judge others, and the amount you give to others will be given to you." (Matthew 7:1–2, NCV)

S—Still growing in their relationship with God

Sponsors need to be living out Principles 7 and 8 on a daily basis. We need to be active in our own recovery.

"Then the way you live will always honor and please the Lord, and your lives will produce every kind of good fruit. All the while, you will grow as you learn to know God better and better." (Colossians 1:10, NLT)

O—Objectivity

Getting too close to the individuals we sponsor can be counterproductive and develop into an unhealthy, codependent relationship.

"So that your daily life may win the respect of outsiders and so that you will not be dependent on anybody." (1 Thessalonians 4:12)

R—Reachable

Sponsors need to be available 24/7 for the individuals they sponsor. We need to be there when the individuals we are sponsoring are going through a crisis.

"And the things you have heard me say in the presence of many witnesses entrust to reliable people who will also be qualified to teach others." (2 Timothy 2:2)

Questions for Reflection and Discussion

1. How has your sponsor helped your with an recent issue? Be specific and provide a detailed account.

2. How many individuals are you currently sponsoring? And what are some of the tools you are using to help and encourage them?

3. How do you rely on God's wisdom to help you be a loving and effective sponsor? Give several examples.

4. Are you comfortable sharing your recovery journey and current struggles with those you sponsor? Are you sponsoring by example? Share some details.

5. How are you continuing to grow in your relationship with God so your own recovery will not suffer?

6. Do you share with the people you sponsor what God is showing you in your daily quiet times? Give some current examples.

7. How do you ensure your relationship with those you sponsor remains healthy and objective? How do you keep it from becoming a codependent relationship?

8. How have you been able to maintain a healthy relationship with your sponsor? Be specific.

9. How do you keep yourself available for those you sponsor who need to reach you in times of crisis? And just as importantly, how do you establish healthy boundaries with those you sponsor?

Prayer

Dear God, thank You for our group. We want to continue to break free from our hurts, hang-ups, and habits, and continue to grow closer to You. Thank You for the leaders You have provided. Thank You that You love us all, no matter where we are in our recovery. Show me the person(s) You have prepared for me to sponsor. Help us to establish an honest and loving relationship that honors You and helps both me and those I sponsor grow stronger in You. In Jesus' name we pray, amen.

Lesson 8

TRUTH

Principle 4: Openly examine and confess my faults to myself, to God, and to someone I trust.

"Happy are the pure in heart." (Matthew 5:8)

Step 4: We made a searching and fearless moral inventory of ourselves.

"Let us examine our ways and test them, and let us return to the LORD." (Lamentations 3:40)

Please begin your time together by reading "A Call for Accountability, Day 107" from the *Celebrate Recovery Daily Devotional.*

In Participant's Guide 2 of *The Journey Begins,* we start the process of taking an honest and spiritual MORAL inventory. We may have done this more than once if we have completed more than one *The Journey Begins* step study. Now in *The Journey Continues*, we are getting ready to do the process again.

To get the most out of this lesson, have your most recent moral inventory (from *The Journey Begins*) available for reference.

Remember, in our inventory we write down all of the good and bad things that we have done and that have been done to us. For many of us, this can be a hard process. You may be wondering, *Why do we need to do this again? Why is this such an important part of recovery?*

Jesus says that, "Then you will know the truth and the truth will set you free" (John 8:32).

When we complete a moral inventory, we begin to see the TRUTH about ourselves. Now that we have been living out our recoveries, how do we continue to find freedom from our hurts, hang-ups, and habits that Jesus promises?

The answer lies in the truth!

TRUTH

T—Take action on any unresolved relational issues from our inventory or on any new issues that have begun

As you look over your last moral inventory, are there any issues that haven't been resolved? Is there anyone you haven't made amends to or offered forgiveness to? Remember that these unresolved relationships are hindering and hurting your recovery—they may even cause your recovery to stall. Ask yourself why you haven't taken the action you need to on these, and call your sponsor or accountability partners/team to ask for their help. Don't leave this to chance. Make a plan on how you will proceed.

"Therefore, if you are offering your gift at the altar and there remember that your brother or sister has something against you, leave your gift there in front of the altar. First go and be reconciled to them; then come and offer your gift." (Matthew 5:23–24)

"Bear with each other and forgive one another if any of you has a grievance against someone. Forgive as the Lord forgave you." (Colossians 3:13)

R—Recognize patterns and behaviors

One way the truth sets us free is by showing us clearly, through the process of the moral inventory, patterns that we may be able to ignore until we see them written on the page.

"I do not understand what I do. For what I want to do I do not do, but what I hate I do. And if I do what I do not want to do, I agree that the law is good. As it is, it is no longer I myself who do it, but it is sin living in me. For I know that good itself does not dwell in me, that is, in my sinful nature. For I have the desire to do what is good, but I cannot carry it out." (Romans 7:15–18)

"Anyone who listens to the word but does not do what it says is like someone who looks at his face in a mirror and, after looking at himself, goes away and immediately forgets what he looks like. But whoever looks intently into the perfect law that gives freedom, and continues in it—not forgetting what they have heard, but doing it—they will be blessed in what they do." (James 1:23–25)

U—Understand that the events in our past shaped us, but they don't define us

Again referencing your latest moral inventory, notice that you were shaped both positively and negatively by the events of your past.

It's in dealing with the events of the past and understanding that they had a hand in making us who we are today, that we are able to face them and then move forward. Denying their impact might feel like freedom, but until we have dealt with them honestly, we will remain trapped by them. We may have done things we regret or things may have been done to us that we wish never happened. Acknowledging their influence, but also trusting that Jesus can use them to help others, takes away their power to define us.

"Therefore, there is now no condemnation for those who are in Christ Jesus." (Romans 8:1)

"I [God], even I, am he who blots out your transgressions, for my own sake, and remembers your sins no more. Review the past for me, let us argue the matter together; state the case for your innocence." (Isaiah 43:25–26)

"Praise be to the God and Father of our Lord Jesus Christ, the Father of compassion and the God of all comfort, who comforts us in all our troubles, so that we can comfort those in any trouble with the comfort we ourselves receive from God." (2 Corinthians 1:3–4)

T—Turn our character defects over to Jesus

Because you are doing a *The Journey Continues* step study, you have already turned your life and at least one recovery issue over to Jesus. You have undoubtedly found freedom over some of the hurts, hang-ups, and habits in your life.

However, if we want to find complete freedom, we need to turn it *all* over to Him. As we have completed a moral inventory and have begun taking a daily inventory, we have most likely observed new character defects other than those that initially brought us to Celebrate Recovery. It is now time to turn those areas over to Jesus as well. After all, we aren't just looking for sobriety but for freedom.

"If we confess our sins, he is faithful and just and will forgive us our sins and purify us from all unrighteousness." (1 John 1:9)

H—Help others along the way

We find freedom when we are able to take the focus off ourselves and put it on helping others. The key in making sure we are doing this in a healthy way is by keeping Jesus at the center of our service. When we help other people, we are directly serving Christ.

"Do nothing out of selfish ambition or vain conceit. Rather, in humility value others above yourselves, not looking to your own interests but each of you to the interests of the others. In your relationships with one another, have the same mindset as Christ Jesus." (Philippians 2:3–5)

Questions for Reflection and Discussion

1. As you prepare to do a new moral inventory, how are you feeling? Excited? Worried? Be specific.

2. Share a lesson you learned from a prior inventory.

3. Review the copy of your most recent inventory. Do you see any relationships or issues that have gone unresolved? If so, what actions do you need to take?

4. What patterns or behaviors did you recognize during your latest inventory? Be specific.

5. How can knowing about those patterns help you as you move forward?

6. What events of your past—both good and bad—have shaped you in big ways? And how does knowing that those events don't define you impact your recovery?

7. How have you used the events of your past to help other people?

8. What character defects have you been unwilling to turn over to Jesus?

9. How can you use what you learned about yourself through the inventory process to help others? Who do you know who needs to hear your story?

Prayer

Heavenly Father, as we begin to complete a new inventory, help us to remember the victories You gave us when we went through The Journey Begins. *We ask that You help us build on that experience and grow deeper in You and in our recoveries. In Your name, amen.*

Lesson 9

INVENTORY

Principle 4: Openly examine and confess my faults to myself, to God, and to someone I trust.

"Happy are the pure in heart." (Matthew 5:8)

Step 4: We made a searching and fearless moral inventory of ourselves.

"Let us examine our ways and test them, and let us return to the LORD." (Lamentations 3:40)

Please begin your time together by reading "The Whole Truth, Day 91" from the *Celebrate Recovery Daily Devotional.*

Let's review: As we said in Lesson 8, it may have been several years since you actually completed your 4th Step Inventory in *The Journey Begins*. You may have discovered over the months or years since you initially completed your inventory that a new struggle or issue has surfaced. So it is important to revisit those inventory sheets once again!

Let's get ready to write. Remember your inventory needs to be on paper. Writing (or typing) will help you organize your thoughts and focus on recalling events that you may have repressed.

Please don't forget, you are not going through this alone. You have developed a strong support team that is here to guide you, but even more importantly, your relationship with Christ has grown significantly since you did your first inventory.

Inventory

Ephesians 4:31 tells us, "Get rid of all bitterness, rage, and anger, brawling and slander, along with every form of malice."

The five-column inventory sheet you used in Participant's Guide 2 of *The Journey Begins* hasn't changed. Why? Because it works. However, there is a *brand new* worksheet called "Pro's from My Inventory" on page 42 for you to write down any victories you have won and/or service you have performed. This is so important! This will help you keep your inventory balanced and help you see all the changes Christ has made in you!

It will take you more than one page to write your inventory. You have permission to copy the "Celebrate Recovery Principle 4 Inventory Worksheet" on pages 40 and 41 and the "Pro's from My Inventory" worksheet on page 42.

Let's review each of the columns:

Column 1: "The Person"

In this column, you list the person or object you resent or fear. You may need to list someone you previously listed in your first step study inventory. You may have a new resentment or issue with them. Remember that resentment is mostly unexpressed anger and fear. Also, list here any new people or objects that have caused you harm, or that you fear or resent, since your last moral inventory.

Column 2: "The Cause"

It has been said that "hurt people hurt people." In this column you are going to list the specific actions that the person did to hurt you. What did the person do to cause you resentment and/or fear? God promises in Isaiah 41:10: "Fear not, for I am with you. Do not be dismayed. I am your God. I will strengthen you; I will help you; I will uphold you with my victorious right hand."

Column 3: "The Effect"

In this column, write down how that specific hurtful action affected your life both in the past and in the present. Or now that some time has passed since your first inventory, if they have hurt you in a new way, how has that affected you?

Column 4: "The Damage"

Which of your basic instincts were injured?

- Social — Have you suffered from broken relationships, slander, or gossip?
- Security — Has your physical safety been threatened? Have you faced financial loss?
- Sexual — Have you been a victim in abusive relationships? Has intimacy or trust been damaged or broken?

No matter how you have been hurt, no matter how lost you may feel, God wants to comfort you and restore you. Remember Ezekiel 34:16, "I will look for those that are lost, I will bring back those that wander off, bandage those that are hurt, and heal those that are sick" (GNT).

Column 5: "My Part"

Lamentations 3:40 states, "Let us examine our ways and test them, and let us return to the LORD." It doesn't say, let us examine *their* ways. You did that already in the first four columns. Now you need to honestly determine the part of the resentment (or any other sin or injury) you are responsible for. Ask God to show you your part in a broken or damaged marriage or relationship, with a distant child or parent, or maybe a job loss. In addition, in this column list all the people whom you have hurt and how you hurt them. (You will use Column 5 later in Principle 6, when you work on becoming willing to make your amends.)

Psalm 139:23–24 tells us, "Examine me, O God, and know my mind; test me, and discover my thoughts. Find out if there is any evil in me and guide me in the everlasting way" (GNT).

> **Please note:** *If you have been in an abusive relationship, especially as a small child, you can find great freedom in this part of the inventory. You see that you had NO part, NO responsibility for the cause of the resentment. By simply writing the words* none *or* not guilty *in Column 5, you can begin to be free from the misplaced shame and guilt you have carried with you. When you first did your inventory, you may have left this out. You may have not wanted to face it. Maybe you physically and mentally could not. Celebrate Recovery has rewritten Step 4 for those who have been sexually or physically abused:*
>
> **Step 4:** Made a searching and fearless moral inventory of ourselves, realizing all wrongs can be forgiven. Renounce the lie that the abuse was our fault.

Before You Begin

Remember the five tools to help you prepare for your inventory:

1. Memorize Isaiah 1:18:

   "Come, let's talk this over!" says the LORD; "no matter how deep the stain of your sins, I can take it out and make you as clean as freshly fallen snow. Even if you are stained as red as crimson, I can make you white as wool!" (Isaiah 1:18, TLB)

2. Read the "Balancing the Scale" verses on page 39.
3. Keep your inventory balanced. List the good as well as the bad. This is very important! As God reveals the good things that you have done in the past, or are doing in the present, list them on the new worksheet, "Pro's from My Inventory" (page 42). You will be amazed to see the growth you have accomplished since your 4th Step Inventory in *The Journey Begins.*

   "For the LORD takes delight in his people; he crowns the humble with victory." (Psalm 149:4)

4. Continue to rely on your support team.
5. Pray continuously.

Don't wait to start your new inventory. Don't believe the lie, "I already did this months or years ago. It's a waste of my time." No, it isn't! It's going to be very important as you continue your journey through Celebrate Recovery. Don't let any obstacle stand in your way!

Questions for Reflection and Discussion

The following questions are for you to share in your *The Journey Continues* group meeting. You still need to share your entire inventory with your sponsor, accountability partner/team, or a person you deem safe.

1. List two of the names (or objects) that you listed in Column 1 of your inventory. Write down a brief history about each of them.

2. Write down specifically what each of the above individuals did or are doing to cause you resentment and/or fear.

3. Write down how each of the above two individual's specific hurtful actions have affected your life both in the past and in the present.

4. Which of your basic instincts were injured or are being injured by the above two individuals? Write down at least three sentences on each individual.

5. Now you need to honestly share your part of the resentment (or any other sin or injury) that you are responsible for regarding the two above individuals. Write down at least three sentences for each individual.

6. Use the new "Pro's from My Inventory" worksheet (page 42) to list three victories and three areas of service you have completed since your most recent inventory in *The Journey Begins.* Write a few sentences on each of them.

Principle 4 Verses

Balancing the Scale

Emotion	**Positive Scripture**
Helplessness	*"For God is at work within you, helping you to want to obey him, and then helping you do what he wants." (Philippians 2:13, TLB)*
Dwelling on the past	*"When someone becomes a Christian, he becomes a brand new person inside. He is not the same anymore. A new life has begun!" (2 Corinthians 5:17, TLB)*
Wanting	*"And it is he who will supply all your needs from his riches in glory, because of what Christ Jesus has done for us." (Philippians 4:19, TLB)*
Loneliness	*Jesus says, "I am with you always." (Matthew 28:20, TLB)*
Oppression, Trouble	*"All who are oppressed may come to him. He is a refuge for them in their times of trouble." (Psalm 9:9, TLB)*
Fear, Doubt	*"Yes, be bold and strong! Banish fear and doubt! For remember, the LORD your God is with you wherever you go." (Joshua 1:9, TLB)*
Melancholy, Apathy	*"This is the day the LORD has made. We will rejoice and be glad in it." (Psalm 118:24, TLB)*
Worry	*"Let him have all your worries and cares, for he is always thinking about you and watching everything that concerns you." (1 Peter 5:7, TLB)*

Celebrate Recovery Principle 4 Inventory Worksheet

1. The Person	2. The Cause	3. The Effect
Who is the object of my resentment or fear?	What specific action did that person take that hurt me?	What effect did that action have on my life?

"Let us examine our ways and test them, and let us return to the LORD." (Lamentations 3:40)

4. The Damage	**5. My Part**
What damage did that action do to my basic social, security, and/or sexual instincts?	What part of the resentment am I responsible for? Who are the people I have hurt? How have I hurt them?

PRO'S FROM MY INVENTORY

"In the same way, let your light shine before others, that they may see your good deeds and glorify your Father in heaven." (Matthew 5:16)

"For the LORD takes delight in his people; he crowns the humble with victory." (Psalm 149:4)

"You, my brothers and sisters, were called to be free. But do not use your freedom to indulge the flesh; rather, serve one another humbly in love." (Galatians 5:13)

VICTORIES	SERVICE

Lesson 10

Spiritual Inventory I

Principle 4: Openly examine and confess my faults to myself, to God, and to someone I trust.

"Happy are the pure in heart." (Matthew 5:8)

Step 4: We made a searching and fearless moral inventory of ourselves.

"Let us examine our ways and test them, and let us return to the LORD." (Lamentations 3:40)

Please begin your time together by reading "Growing Up, Day 89" from the *Celebrate Recovery Daily Devotional.*

Before you begin this exercise, find Lesson 10 (Participant's Guide 2) from the previous *The Journey Begins* step studies. Use it as a reference to what you wrote in your first or most recent moral inventory. This time, challenge yourself to dig deeper, to look past your main recovery issue and ask yourself some hard questions. Your first inventory was likely focused on your main recovery issue, the thing that brought you to Celebrate Recovery in the first place. Now, try to see if any secondary issues may have revealed themselves. This doesn't mean that you should ignore your primary issue or leave things off this inventory, but it does mean you should see if anything *new* needs your attention.

To help get started on your new inventory, here are some key areas that deserve examination.

Relationships

Those we have hurt

The Bible says, "For all have sinned and fall short of the glory of God" (Romans 3:23). This means that we've all been hurt by others, and we have all hurt others with our actions. Remember, you don't need to go all the way back to before you began recovery. Instead, focus on issues that may have come up since your last moral inventory.

Who has been hurt by your actions?

Have you hurt anyone and feel like you are beyond forgiveness?

What actions can you take to make it right?

(**Note:** The people who you name in these areas will go in Column 1 of your Celebrate Recovery Inventory Worksheet.)

People who have hurt us

Are you still holding a grudge or seeking revenge against anyone?

Who are you unwilling to forgive?

(**Note:** The people who you name in these areas will go in Column 5 of your Celebrate Recovery Inventory Worksheet.)

Priorities

The desires of our heart reveal what we love. "For where your treasure is, there your heart will be also" (Luke 12:34).

What things have you put above God or His people?

What have you held back and not turned over to Jesus?

In what ways are you still following *your* will instead of *God's* will?

Attitude

The Bible says, "Rejoice always, pray continually, give thanks in all circumstances; for this is God's will for you in Christ Jesus" (1 Thessalonians 5:16–18).

How do you see your circumstances today?

Have you cultivated an "attitude of gratitude" or do you grumble and complain?

Are you worried? Are you anxious?

How is your temper?

Do you use anger, intimidation, or sarcasm to manipulate people?

Integrity

Are you the same person at church and out in the world?

Do you pretend you have it all together?

At the end of the day do you regret how you acted?

Questions for Reflection and Discussion

Your Relationships

1. Is there anyone from a prior moral inventory who you haven't forgiven?

2. Is there anyone from a prior moral inventory to whom you have not made amends?

3. What is holding you back?

4. Has anyone hurt you recently? Has this person hurt you in the past? Is this a pattern?

5. Who have you hurt recently?

6. Did you make amends when you realized you hurt them? Did you do it promptly?

7. What were your motives when you hurt them? Did you hurt them intentionally or by accident? How does that make a difference?

Your Priorities

8. What's the most important thing in your life, right now? How has that changed since you started Celebrate Recovery?

9. Is there anything in your life that you haven't turned over to God's control?

10. Is there anything in your life that you're willing to compromise your morals to achieve?

11. What do you spend most of your time doing?

Your Attitude

12. What do you complain about? What are you grateful for today?

13. Do you ever compare your situation to the situations of others?

14. What would your loved ones or your sponsor say is your main character trait?

15. When's the last time you really lost your temper? How did you respond?

16. Do you ever find yourself thinking, "This isn't fair"? What about?

Your Integrity

17. Do you ever find yourself acting differently depending on the people you are with?

18. Would others look at your life and see that you have grown since starting Celebrate Recovery?

19. Is the "you" you present online and in social media the same as the "you" in real life?

20. Does your walk match your talk? How?

Lesson 11

Spiritual Inventory 2

Principle 4: Openly examine and confess my faults to myself, to God, and to someone I trust.

"Happy are the pure in heart." (Matthew 5:8)

Step 4: We made a searching and fearless moral inventory of ourselves.

"Let us examine our ways and test them, and let us return to the Lord." (Lamentations 3:40)

Please begin your time together by reading "The Trouble with Grudges, Day 92" from the *Celebrate Recovery Daily Devotional.*

As in the last lesson, let's take a look at four more areas to help us write our updated moral inventory. Remember to seek God and ask Him to reveal any areas in your life that you need to turn over to Him.

Mind

"Since, then, you have been raised with Christ, set your hearts on things above, where Christ is, seated at the right hand of God. Set your minds on things above, not on earthly things." (Colossians 3:1–2)

Do you find yourself thinking about, or fantasizing about, your life before recovery?

What do you think about most often?

Would you say you spend more time thinking about earthly things or heavenly things?

What negative or hurtful things are you allowing into your mind?

Are you filling your mind with healthy things, such as Bible reading?

Body

"Therefore do not let sin reign in your mortal body so that you obey its evil desires. Do not offer any part of yourself to sin as an instrument of wickedness, but rather offer yourselves to God as those who have been brought from death to life; and offer every part of yourself to him as an instrument of righteousness." (Romans 6:12–13)

"Each of you should learn to control your own body in a way that is holy and honorable." (1 Thessalonians 4:4)

What are you doing to take care of the body God has given you?

What positive lifestyle changes have you made since starting recovery?

Are there still ways you are mistreating your body?

Family

"Choose for yourselves this day whom you will serve.... But as for me and my household, we will serve the LORD." (Joshua 24:15)

How has your attitude toward your family changed since starting Celebrate Recovery?

Have you offered forgiveness or made amends to the members of your family?

How do you see the events of your childhood today?

Church

"And let us consider how we may spur one another on toward love and good deeds, not giving up meeting together, as some are in the habit of doing, but encouraging one another—and all the more as you see the Day approaching." (Hebrews 10:24–25)

Are you currently serving at your church?

Are you making church attendance a priority?

Do you ever find yourself complaining about your family's involvement at church?

Questions for Reflection and Discussion

Your Mind

1. What are you filling your mind with?

2. Do you read, watch, or listen to anything that is harmful?

3. If someone found your browser history, would you be embarrassed?

4. In what ways have you filled your mind with positive things?

5. What is the last Bible verse you memorized?

Your Body

6. What are you doing to protect your physical health?

7. Have you started any new habits that are negatively affecting your body?

8. Have you started any new habits that are positively affecting your body?

9. How are you honoring Christ with your body?

10. How have decisions you've made in the past affected your physical well-being?

Your Family

11. How are you showing the love of Christ to your family?

12. How has your recovery changed the way you relate to your family?

13. Are there members of your family whom you have not forgiven? How is this affecting your recovery?

14. How have making amends and offering forgiveness to your family members impacted your recovery?

15. How are you encouraging the members of your family to find the help they need?

16. Can those in your family see the changes God has made in you? How?

Your Church

17. Are you serving in a local church? If so, how? If not, why not?

18. What are some ways you invite your friends and family to church so they can find the healing you have found?

19. When you see a problem in your church or in your Celebrate Recovery ministry, do you offer a solution or do you complain?

20. How are you praying for your pastor and Celebrate Recovery leaders?

21. How can you better serve Christ through your church?

AFTERWORD

Congratulations on completing a brand new inventory! While it was a lot of work, you can be sure God is going to do some big things because of your dedication to see it through. While completing your new inventory, you may have discovered a few things. First, you may have noticed that you are still struggling with an old hurt, hang-up, or habit for which you thought you had found victory. Or, you may have found a new issue that you had not previously identified. It might be that certain people appeared on this inventory to whom you still need to make amends or offer forgiveness.

In any of these cases, be ready take the next steps to help you find true freedom. In Participant's Guide 7, *Honoring God by Making Repairs*, you will continue the process of doing your part to make relationships right and take a deeper look at some key areas in your life.

But before you move on, spend a few more minutes reflecting on your "Pro's from My Inventory" worksheet. Be encouraged by how, through God's guidance and your positive efforts, you have continued to grow!

You've done some great work so far; keep it up as you move forward on your recovery journey!

ALSO AVAILABLE

CELEBRATE RECOVERY 30 ANNIVERSARY

NIV Celebrate Recovery® Study Bible

The *NIV Celebrate Recovery Study Bible* is a powerful and positive ally. This Bible is based on eight recovery principles found in Jesus' Sermon on the Mount and on the underlying Christ-centered twelve steps of the proven Celebrate Recovery program. Now typeset in Zondervan's exclusive Comfort Print® typeface, this Bible and all of its added content lifts you up and shows you how to walk, step by attainable step, on a path of healing and liberty.

Features:

- The full text of the accurate, readable, and clear New International Version (NIV) translation
- Articles explain eight recovery principles and accompanying Christ-centered twelve steps
- 110 lessons unpack eight recovery principles in practical terms
- Recovery stories offer encouragement and hope
- 30 days of recovery-related readings
- Over 50 full-page biblical character studies are tied to stories from real-life people who have found peace and help with their own hurts, hang-ups, and habits
- Book introductions
- Side-column reference system keyed to Celebrate Recovery's eight recovery principles
- Topical index
- Exclusive Zondervan NIV Comfort Print typeface in 9-point print size

9780310455257

Available now at your favorite bookstore.

ZONDERVAN®

ALSO AVAILABLE

CELEBRATE RECOVERY
30
ANNIVERSARY

Your First Step to Celebrate Recovery®

Author and founder John Baker tells the story of how Celebrate Recovery® became one of the largest Christ-centered recovery programs in history. Baker will help you discover how God's love, truth, grace, and forgiveness can heal your hurts, hang-ups, and habits. Available individually or as a six-copy pack.

Individual Book
9780310125440

6-Pack
9780310125457

Available now at your favorite bookstore.

ZONDERVAN®

ALSO AVAILABLE

CELEBRATE RECOVERY 30 ANNIVERSARY

Celebrate Recovery®

365 DAILY DEVOTIONAL

This daily devotional is specially designed to complement the Celebrate Recovery® program. It features 366 brief original readings, each a powerful reminder of God's goodness, grace, and redemption and an inspiration to anyone struggling with old hurts, habits, and hang-ups. The *Celebrate Recovery 365 Daily Devotional* will encourage everyone who is on the road to recovery.

9780310458845

Available now at your favorite bookstore.

ZONDERVAN®

ALSO AVAILABLE

CELEBRATE RECOVERY 30 ANNIVERSARY

Celebrate Recovery®
JOURNAL

Specifically tied to the eight recovery principles of the Celebrate Recovery® program, the *Celebrate Recovery Journal* is specially designed to help you go through the recovery process step-by-step. Includes tips on how to benefit from journaling, Scriptures pulled from the Celebrate Recovery program, and a 90-day review.

9780310136231

Available now at your favorite bookstore.

ZONDERVAN®

ALSO AVAILABLE

CELEBRATE RECOVERY 30 ANNIVERSARY

Celebrate Recovery®

THE JOURNEY CONTINUES

PARTICIPANT'S GUIDES 5-8

Celebrate Recovery® introduces *The Journey Continues*—four participant's guides designed as a revolutionary, second step study curriculum. This step study is taken after completing *The Journey Begins* (Participant Guides 1-4). By working through the lessons and exercises found in each of the four participant's guides of *The Journey Continues* you will find a deeper sense of true peace and serenity, continue to restore and develop stronger relationships with others and with God, and find deeper freedom from life's hurts, habits, and hang-ups.

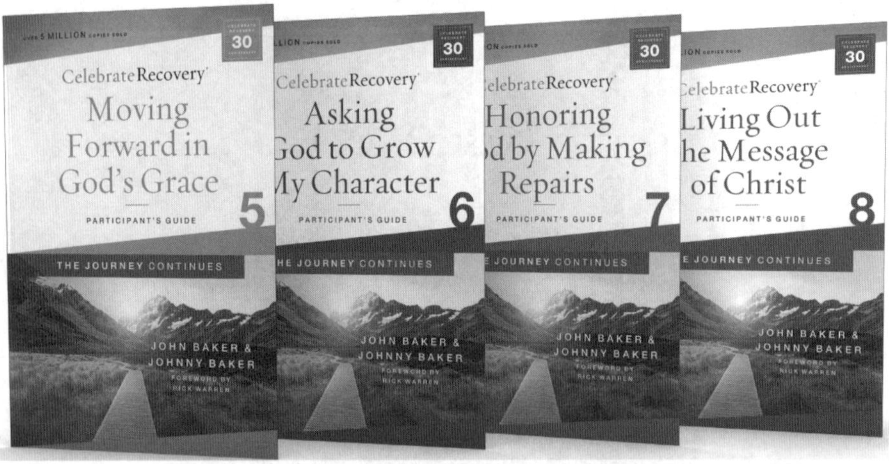

9780310131465 9780310131489 9780310131502 9780310131526

Available now at your favorite bookstore.

ZONDERVAN®